THE BIGGEST (and Best) FLAG THAT EVER FLEW

By Rebecca C. Jones

ILLUSTRATED BY CHARLES GEER

Tidewater Publishers : Centreville, Maryland

CAROLINE PICKERSGILL lived with her mother
and grandmother in a small house on Albemarle Street
in Baltimore. Caroline's father had died, and her
mother worked at home, making flags—bright, colorful
flags for the ships that sailed into Baltimore Harbor.

Mrs. Pickersgill made many different kinds of flags
for ships from all over the world, but the flags that
Caroline liked best were the flags that flew over the

American ships. They had fifteen stars and fifteen stripes,
for the first fifteen states in the United States of America.

Sometimes Caroline went to the harbor with her
mother. She liked to see all of the flags and banners
waving in the breeze. But she worried when she heard
people talk about the war with Great Britain. They said

4

the British troops wanted to destroy Baltimore. They wanted to burn everything, even the little house on Albemarle Street.

"Don't worry," Caroline's mother said on the way home. "The British won't burn Baltimore. The soldiers at Fort McHenry will protect us."

Caroline knew the soldiers at Fort McHenry had many guns and big cannons to protect the people of Baltimore. So she tried not to worry, even when she heard people say that the British had even more guns and even bigger cannons.

One day some soldiers from Fort McHenry came to Caroline's house to talk to her mother. They wanted Mrs. Pickersgill to sew the biggest and best flag she had ever

sewn. They wanted it to be the biggest flag in the whole world, big enough so everyone could see it from far away and know that Baltimore was safe.

The soldiers needed the flag right away so Caroline
and her mother started working at once. They worked
upstairs in Mrs. Pickersgill's bedroom, cutting and
sewing, until after midnight every night.

They made each red or white stripe as wide as the
widest cloth they could find. They wanted the stars even
wider, so Mrs. Pickersgill had to weave them herself.

They didn't have enough room in their little house
to put the big flag together. So Caroline and her mother
carried the stars and stripes to a big building down the
street.

They spread the pieces out on the floor, and they
sewed the huge red and white stripes together. Then they
laid out the wide white stars on the dark blue background
and sewed them in place.

Finally, the flag was finished. It was thirty feet wide
and forty-two feet long, and it weighed 200 pounds.
Nobody had ever seen such a big and beautiful flag.

When the soldiers saw the flag, they were very pleased. "No one will have trouble seeing this flag," they said. "And everyone will know Baltimore is safe."

The soldiers took the flag to Fort McHenry and
raised it up a big pole there.

Three miles away, from an upstairs window in their
house, Caroline and her mother could see the flag. They
were sure it was the biggest—and best—flag in the world.

Everybody kept talking about the war. The British
had just captured Washington, the capital of the country,
only thirty miles from Baltimore. They had burned the
Capitol building and the White House, where the
president lived. Everyone said they would attack
Baltimore next.

And they did. On a rainy September morning,
British ships fired on Fort McHenry. The soldiers at the
fort fired back.

Caroline and her mother hurried to the attic window to watch the battle. They looked for their flag, but they couldn't see anything in the rain and the mist. They could only hear the thunder of the guns and cannons.

Some of their neighbors began packing their belongings so they could leave Baltimore before the British burned it. But Caroline and her mother stayed in

their house on Albemarle Sreet, and the battle continued
through the night.

In the morning they hurried back to the window to see if their big flag was flying.

It was.

The British had given up, and Baltimore was safe.

That afternoon Caroline heard about a young American lawyer named Francis Scott Key who had been on a ship in the harbor during the battle. He too had watched for the flag, and he had written a poem about it.

Oh, say, can you see
  by the dawn's early light,
What so proudly we hailed
  at the twilight's last gleaming?
Whose broad stripes and bright stars,
  through the perilous fight,
O'er the ramparts we watched
  were so gallantly streaming?
And the rockets' red glare,
  the bombs bursting in air,
Gave proof through the night
  that our flag was still there.
Oh, say, does that star-spangled banner
  yet wave
O'er the land of the free
  and the home of the brave?

Today that poem is our national anthem, and we sing it at ball games, special ceremonies, and public events—whenever we want to honor the American flag.

And the huge flag—the one that was too big for Caroline Pickersgill's house on Albemarle Street—is now the biggest (and maybe the best) exhibit in the Smithsonian Institution's National Museum of American History in Washington, D.C.